W9-BSY-036

# Humanitarian Organizations

# Greenpeace

Ann Parry

**CHELSEA HOUSE**
PUBLISHERS

A Haights Cross Communications ✈ Company ®

Philadelphia

*For Jack and Win Parry—exceptional and loving parents.*

This edition first published in 2006 in the United States of America by Chelsea House Publishers, a subsidiary of Haights Cross Communications.

A Haights Cross Communications ✦ Company ®

Chelsea House Publishers
2080 Cabot Boulevard West, Suite 201
Langhorne, PA 19047-1813

The Chelsea House world wide web address is www.chelseahouse.com

First published in 2005 by
MACMILLAN EDUCATION AUSTRALIA PTY LTD
627 Chapel Street, South Yarra 3141

Visit our website at www.macmillan.com.au

Associated companies and representatives throughout the world.

Copyright © Ann Parry 2005

Library of Congress Cataloging-in-Publication Data applied for.
ISBN 0 7910 8815 4

Edited by Angelique Campbell-Muir and Anna Fern
Cover and text design by Raul Diche
Maps by Pat Kermode
Photo research by Legend Images

Printed in China

**Acknowledgments**

The author and publisher are grateful to Greenpeace for its assistance and advice in the preparation of this book.

The author and the publisher are also grateful to the following for permission to reproduce copyright material:

Cover photographs: Greenpeace activists, courtesy of Greenpeace/Cunningham. Greenpeace's hot-air balloon protest over the Taj Mahal, courtesy of Greenpeace/Morgan. Greenpeace forest campaigners, courtesy of Greenpeace.

Amnesty International, p. 4 (logo); Australian Red Cross, p. 4 (logo); Doctors Without Borders/Médecins Sans Frontières (MSF), p. 4 (logo); Greenpeace, pp. 4 (logo), 5, 8, 11, 17, 22, 26, 30; Greenpeace/Dave Adair, pp. 19, 23; Greenpeace/Barry, p. 14; Greenpeace/Bradley, p. 16; Greenpeace/Cobbing, p. 28; Greenpeace/Cole, pp. 10, 25; Greenpeace/Cunningham, p. 20; Greenpeace/Davison, p. 27; Greenpeace/Keziere, p. 9; Greenpeace/Morgan, pp. 1, 15; Greenpeace/Karen Robinson, p. 29; Greenpeace/Scheltema, p. 24; Greenpeace/Sewell, p. 21; Greenpeace/Taylor, p. 18; Greenpeace/Weyler, p. 6; Newspix, p. 7; the Peace Corps, p. 4 (logo); Save the Children, p. 4 (logo).

While every care has been taken to trace and acknowledge copyright, the publisher tenders their apologies for any accidental infringement where copyright has proved untraceable. Where the attempt has been unsuccessful, the publisher welcomes information that would redress the situation.

**Please note**
At the time of printing, the Internet addresses appearing in this book were correct. Owing to the dynamic nature of the Internet, however, we cannot guarantee that all these addresses will remain correct.

# Contents

What is a humanitarian organization?     4

About Greenpeace     5

History of Greenpeace     6

The founders of Greenpeace     8

Early work     9

Core values of Greenpeace     10

Where in the world is Greenpeace?     12

Timeline     13

Concerns, campaigns, and classic actions     14

    Nuclear threats to the future     15

    Genetically engineered food     16

    The destruction of old-growth forests     17

    Climate change     18

    Toxic damage     19

    The health of the world's oceans     20

    The increasing number of wars and conflicts     21

The people of Greenpeace     22

CLEMENS TOLUSSO   Toxics campaigner     22

VANESSA ATKINSON   Climate campaigner     24

HENRY TINDIPE   Forest campaigner     26

LOUISE EDGE   Press officer     28

What can you do?     30

Glossary     31

Index     32

**Glossary words**

When a word is printed in **bold**, its meaning is included on that page. You can also look up its meaning in the Glossary on page 31.

# What is a humanitarian organization?

**H**umanitarian organizations work to help solve problems in countries around the world, wherever there is a need for their help. They are sometimes called aid agencies, non-profit, or non-governmental organizations (NGOs). Some organizations, such as Greenpeace, work to protect the environment. Others, such as Amnesty International and the International Red Cross, work to protect people's **human rights** or provide for their basic needs in times of conflict and disaster. Doctors Without Borders sends **volunteers** anywhere in the world to give medical help to people affected by disasters. Groups like Save the Children and Australian Volunteers International help rebuild communities who need food, education, and advice.

Some humanitarian organizations are given money by governments to help run their programs. They also work hard to collect enough money from the public to keep going. Some of their workers are volunteers and are not paid, while others work for a small wage.

The *Humanitarian Organizations* series focuses on six well-known organizations and explains how they help those in need around the world.

## Glossary words

**humanitarian**
devoted to people's welfare and the promotion of social reform

**human rights**
a set of rights, such as the right to a fair trial, laid down by the United Nations

**volunteers**
people who donate their time to a cause

*The Peace Corps*

*The Red Cross*

*Greenpeace*

*Save the Children*

*Amnesty International*

*Doctors Without Borders*

# About Greenpeace

Greenpeace is an independent organization that is not like other aid agencies. Greenpeace is different because it aims to "ensure a just, peaceful, sustainable environment for future generations." The name "Greenpeace" was chosen to show the organization's hope for a green and peaceful world. Bill Darnell, one of the organization's founding members, suggested joining the two words to show the group's concern for the Earth and opposition to nuclear weapons.

## Greenpeace policy

Behind the scenes, Greenpeace campaigns on many levels. Its policy is to use nonviolent, direct actions to expose global environmental problems and to force solutions. Some of the actions taken in Greenpeace campaigns have been quite spectacular and have received worldwide publicity.

## Consequences

Some Greenpeace **activists** have been arrested while making protests, and some have even spent time in jail. These Greenpeace members are prepared to do this because they believe it is the only way that the environmental problems of the world can be made public and eventually be solved.

*Glossary words*

**activists**
people who take direct action for a cause

**glacial retreat**
the increased melting of glaciers due to climate change

**global warming**
the gradual increase in temperatures across the Earth, largely caused by too much carbon dioxide in the atmosphere

The icefields in Patagonia are suffering from the fastest **glacial retreat** on Earth caused by **global warming**.

*This is the logo for Greenpeace.*

# History of Greenpeace

In 1971, a small team of activists set sail from Vancouver, Canada, in an old fishing boat. They were heading for a group of islands off the west coast of Alaska called the Aleutians, in one of the world's most earthquake-prone regions.

The Phyllis Cormack *was used to transport members for Greenpeace's first action.*

## Amchitka

At that time, the government of the United States of America was performing underground testing of nuclear weapons at one of the islands, called Amchitka. Amchitka was the last refuge for 3,000 endangered sea otters. It was also home to bald eagles, peregrine falcons, and other wildlife.

## Bearing witness

The founders of Greenpeace believed that even a few individuals could make a difference. Their mission was to "bear witness" to the testing. This meant they would let people know about what was happening, so that people who wanted to could speak out against it.

## Publicity success

Even though their old boat, the *Phyllis Cormack*, was stopped before she got to Amchitka, the journey got a lot of publicity. The United States of America still detonated their bomb, but the activists had made people aware of the incident.

Nuclear testing on Amchitka ended that same year, and the island was later declared a bird sanctuary.

Did you know?

The *Phyllis Cormack* was later renamed the *Greenpeace*.

## Early actions

Later in the 1970s, this tiny new organization protested against the slaughter of baby harp seals in Newfoundland. They also sailed their new ship, the *Vega*, to an island called Muroroa, in the

*The Greenpeace ships* Vega *(left),* The Love of Gaia *(center) and the* Rainbow Warrior *(right) sail to Australia to protest the unloading of genetically engineered soybeans.*

South Pacific, to protest against French nuclear testing. Greenpeace generated a lot of publicity about both of these events and, in both cases, the governments involved changed their policies.

In 1981, Greenpeace had another victory when the **International Whaling Commission** (IWC) banned the hunting of sperm whales. Other early Greenpeace actions included campaigns against dumping toxic waste, offshore oil drilling, and pollution from power plants.

## The bombing of the *Rainbow Warrior*

In 1985, in Auckland Harbour, New Zealand, the Greenpeace flagship, the *Rainbow Warrior*, was bombed by French Secret Service agents trying to stop the anti-nuclear campaign. Photographer Fernando Pereira was killed and the bombing caused headlines around the world, but Greenpeace was not intimidated. More campaigns were launched and more members joined.

## Greenpeace today

Today, Greenpeace is a global organization fighting to solve environmental problems. It is based in Amsterdam, with 2.65 million supporters worldwide, and has national and regional offices in 41 countries.

*Glossary word*

**International Whaling Commission**
the international group of governments responsible for protecting whales and managing whaling

Did you know?

The name of the Greenpeace flagship, *Rainbow Warrior*, comes from a Cree Native American legend. It describes a time when the human race's greed made the Earth sick. At that time, a tribe of people known as the Warriors of the Rainbow would rise up to defend her.

# The founders of Greenpeace

In 1969, the American Atomic Energy Commission exploded a nuclear bomb on the tiny island of Amchitka, near Alaska, in one of the worst earthquake regions in the world. Many people were afraid, because five years earlier an earthquake in Alaska had sent waves crashing onto beaches as far away as Japan.

On the day of the blast, 10,000 protestors blocked the major American–Canadian border crossing, waving a banner that read: "Don't Make a Wave. It's Your Fault if Our Fault Goes." The American government ignored the protests and announced plans for another test in 1971.

*Some of the founding members of Greenpeace on board the* Phyllis Cormack *to protest against nuclear testing.*

## Don't Make a Wave Committee

In 1970, the Don't Make a Wave Committee was established. Its plan was to stop the second test planned for 1971. The committee's first members included:

- Paul Cote, a law student at the University of British Columbia
- Jim Bohlen, a former deep-sea diver and radar operator in the United States Navy
- Irving Stowe, a lawyer and a member of the Quaker religion
- Patrick Moore, an **ecology** student at the University of British Columbia
- Bill Darnell, a social worker.

*Glossary word*

**ecology**
the science of living things and their surroundings

Did you know?

One hundred and fifteen people were killed as a result of an earthquake in Alaska in 1964.

# Early work

Greenpeace's first action was to "bear witness" to the nuclear test on Amchitka. On board the *Phyllis Cormack* for that first journey were:

- Captain John Cormack, the boat's owner
- Dr. Jim Bohlen, Bill Darnell, and Patrick Moore, Greenpeace members
- Lyle Thurston, doctor
- Dave Birmingham, engineer
- Terry Simmons, geographer
- Richard Fineberg, teacher
- Robert Hunter, Ben Metcalfe, and Bob Cummings, journalists
- Bob Keziere, photographer.

The other founding members, Irving Stowe and Paul Cote, stayed behind. Stowe suffered from sea sickness and stayed on shore to organize a group of people to try to influence politicians. Cote was about to represent Canada in an Olympic sailing race.

The voyage to Amchitka made the name Greenpeace known in Canada. Greenpeace's next journey, to Muroroa, made it known around the world.

**Five months after the voyage to Amchitka on the *Phyllis Cormack*, the American government announced an end to nuclear tests in the Aleutian Islands "for political and other reasons."**

*The Greenpeace sail is raised on the* Phyllis Cormack *as it sails to Amchitka.*

9

# Core values of Greenpeace

Core values are the things that a person, group, or organization really believes in. The values are used to work out rules of behavior. Greenpeace has three core values: independence, bearing witness, and nonviolent direct action.

## Independence

Greenpeace does not accept money from governments, businesses, or political parties. By not accepting their money, Greenpeace is not influenced by any sponsors.

## Bearing witness

This is an idea from the Quaker religion. It means that Greenpeace uses peaceful protests to raise public awareness of environmental crimes and to bring pressure on decision makers. Greenpeace lets perpetrators know, in a nonviolent way, that their actions are being observed.

## Nonviolent direct action

Greenpeace strongly believes that violence in any form is morally wrong and achieves nothing. Greenpeace also believes, however, that sometimes rules such as "No trespassing" might need to be broken if it means protecting the environment for the future. David McTaggart (1932–2001), the founder of Greenpeace International, once said: "You're trying to get your children into the 21st century. To hell with the rules."

**Did you know?**

One of the longest Greenpeace banners ever made said: "When the last tree is cut, the last river poisoned, and the last fish dead, we will discover that we can't eat money."

*This message of peace was projected onto the Sydney Harbour Bridge in 2003.*

*Greenpeace activists in Tasmania voice their opinion on illegal fishing.*

## Other values

Greenpeace workers believe in being brave enough to confront people who damage the Earth. They try to plan clever public protests which attract people's attention. They also try to maintain high standards of behavior. They encourage others to join them in taking action so that people can feel **empowered** to protect their world.

While direct actions gain lots of publicity, Greenpeace carries out its work in other ways as well.

### Researching

Working with international experts, Greenpeace researches the causes and effects of environmental pollution in order to find solutions.

### Lobbying (convincing powerful people to help)

Greenpeace campaigners regularly meet with governments and industries to make sure the environment is always considered when making decisions.

### Spreading the word

A strong media and communications team makes sure the voice of Greenpeace is heard around the world.

### Working together

Greenpeace forms partnerships with other non-governmental organizations, including working with local group members of such organizations. For example, in the Pacific, Greenpeace helps local owners of the coastal resources and forests that are under threat. They work together to plan alternative, sustainable methods of development.

In 1995, more than seven million people signed petitions calling for a stop to nuclear testing.

*Glossary word*

**empowered**
given the power to make something happen

# Where in the world is Greenpeace?

Greenpeace works in many countries around the world. This map shows where some major Greenpeace campaigns are located.

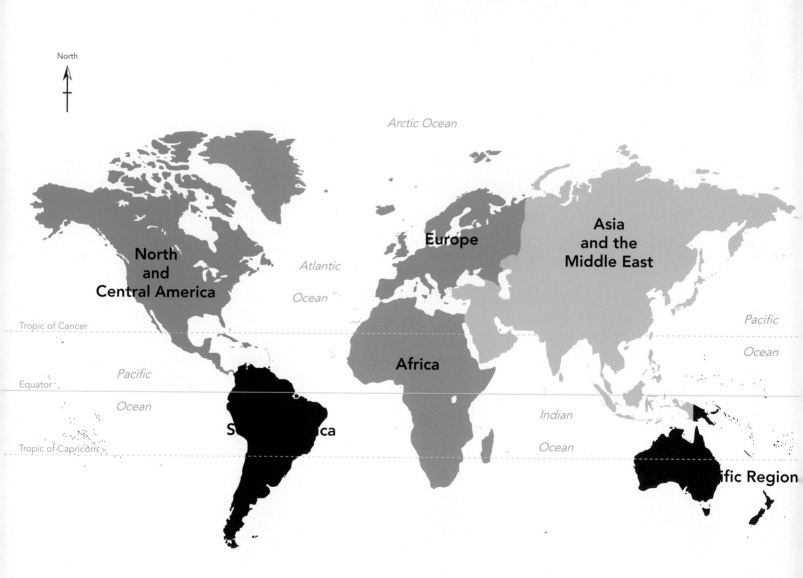

North

Arctic Ocean

Europe

Asia and the Middle East

North and Central America

Atlantic Ocean

Pacific Ocean

Tropic of Cancer

Pacific Ocean

Africa

Equator

S        ica

Indian Ocean

Tropic of Capricorn

ific Region

Southern Ocean

12

# Timeline

Greenpeace has been working to help people since it began in 1970.

## Key to countries

**PACIFIC REGION**
Australia, Fiji, French Polynesia, New Zealand, Papua New Guinea

**ASIA AND THE MIDDLE EAST**
China, India, Israel, Japan, Lebanon, Philippines, Thailand

**EUROPE**
Austria, Belgium, Czech Republic, Denmark, Finland, France, Germany, Greece, Hungary, Italy, Luxembourg, Malta, Netherlands, Norway, Poland, Russian Federation, Slovakia, Spain, Sweden, Switzerland, Turkey, United Kingdom

**AFRICA**
Tunisia

**NORTH AND CENTRAL AMERICA**
Alaska, Canada, Mexico, United States of America

**SOUTH AMERICA**
Argentina, Brazil, Chile

|  |  |
|------|-------|
| 1969 | First nuclear test is conducted at Amchitka. |
| 1970 | Don't Make a Wave Committee is founded, which is the beginning of Greenpeace. |
| 1971 | United States of America abandons nuclear testing at Amchitka after the first major Greenpeace action. |
| 1982 | International Whaling Commission adopts a moratorium, or postponement, on whaling. |
| 1985 | *Rainbow Warrior* is blown up in New Zealand. |
| 1989 | United Nations, an organization of representatives from many countries, declares a moratorium on the large-scale use of driftnets for fishing in the high seas. |
| 1996 | United Nations adopts the Comprehensive Nuclear Test Ban Treaty. A treaty is a formal signed agreement between countries. |
| 1997 | Most industrial nations (except the United States of America and Australia) sign the Kyoto Protocol, a binding international agreement to reduce greenhouse gases. |
| 2000 | G8 adopts Greenpeace's demands to fight illegal logging. (G8 is a group of major industrial countries, (including France, USA, Britain, Germany, Japan, Italy, Canada, and Russia) who meet to discuss business and political issues once a year.) |
| 2003 | At a meeting in Berlin, the International Whaling Commission (IWC) agrees to make conservation central to its work and to help protect the world's whales, dolphins, and porpoises. |
| 2004 | The Australian government agrees to abide by the Stockholm Convention, an international treaty that bans 12 of the most toxic chemicals ever produced. |

# Concerns, campaigns, and classic actions

Greenpeace is involved in several major campaigns on issues affecting the environment. While most Greenpeace activists work on problems specific to their own region, some also travel to international meetings to **lobby** on environmental issues.

Major Greenpeace campaigns include:

- supporting **nuclear disarmament** and finding alternatives to the nuclear industry
- banning **genetically modified organisms** and eliminating genetically engineered food
- protecting the old forests and supporting other ways for people to make a living
- avoiding climate change by phasing out the use of **fossil fuels** and replacing them with clean **renewable energy**
- eliminating toxins such as pesticides and industrial chemicals, and preventing the dumping of dangerous waste
- protecting the oceans from over-fishing and whaling.

Each campaign covers several smaller issues and each campaign keeps to Greenpeace's core values of independence, bearing witness, and nonviolent direct action.

### Glossary words

**lobby**
to attempt to convince government, business, or other powerful groups to change their policy or practices

**nuclear disarmament**
removal of all nuclear weapons and the facilities that make them

**genetically modified organisms**
living things that have had their genetic structure changed

**fossil fuels**
sources of energy from the ground, such as coal, gas, and oil

**renewable energy**
an energy source that will not run out, such as sunlight or wind

*Greenpeace is opposed to the development of more fossil fuel industries because they are a threat to the environment.*

As of January 2002, 2.8 million Greenpeace members had taken out or renewed their financial membership within the previous 18 months. Financial support keeps Greenpeace ships on the oceans and campaigners in the field. There are also millions of cyberactivists and volunteers.

# Nuclear threats to the future

Greenpeace is concerned about nuclear threats to the future. It does not believe that any nuclear reactor can ever be completely safe from an accident. Greenpeace is also concerned about the build-up of dangerous nuclear waste when it is transported through cities and when it is stored, and believes it is a threat to people's lives and to the environment.

## CAMPAIGNS

In the 20th century, some countries began to rely on nuclear reactors for their power supply, and sometimes as part of their defense programs.

The Greenpeace campaigns against nuclear threats aim for a complete end to all nuclear reactors, nuclear power, **reprocessing**, and waste dumping, and want nuclear threats replaced with non-radioactive alternatives. Greenpeace activists keep watch on the transport of waste from nuclear reactors and inform the public about such events. They protest outside companies involved in nuclear research. They also encourage people to write to their governments demanding changes to the laws supporting the nuclear industry.

## Classic action

Greenpeace has organized what are now historic hot-air balloon flights as a protest against nuclear testing. These include flights over the American nuclear test site in Nevada, in 1987, and over the Taj Mahal, in India, in 1998.

*Greenpeace's hot-air balloon protest over the Taj Mahal attracted a lot of attention.*

*Glossary word*

**reprocessing**
separation of plutonium from used-up nuclear fuel

# Genetically engineered food

Greenpeace is concerned that genetic engineering in our food may lead to unplanned and unexpected consequences. Greenpeace believes that we do not yet know enough about the effects it may have on the environment and on human health, and that once these changes begin they cannot be turned back.

## CAMPAIGNS

Genes are the building blocks for all living things. Scientists have discovered ways of altering genes in many life forms. In animals and plants, genes are altered to produce bigger, disease-free varieties that are better for the market.

Greenpeace believes that genetically modified (GM) food is not safe, and campaigns

*Greenpeace activists dressed as chickens in a peaceful protest against genetically engineered foods.*

to have all such food labeled. It also wants all GM crops kept separate from conventional ones. Greenpeace has produced a *True Food Guide* to deliver information to the community. It has also produced a Genetic Engineering Action Kit for concerned people to use to try to encourage such groups as councils and school menus to avoid GM food.

## Classic action

In New Zealand, a group of women called MAdGE (Mothers Against Genetic Engineering) operates a website to inform people about GM food, and to minimize or prevent GM food from being sold in their country.

# The destruction of old-growth forests

Greenpeace is concerned that the few old-growth forests left in the world, such as those in Papua New Guinea, are being ruined by both legal and illegal industrial logging. Although landowners earn money from the logging, it is only a small percentage of the value of the logs that are taken. Greenpeace is particularly concerned because once these forests are logged, they can never be the same again. In some cases, the plants and animals that live in them can be in danger of becoming extinct.

## CAMPAIGNS

Greenpeace makes public the effects logging can have on water supplies, hunting and fishing, and on plants that are used in traditional medicine. It encourages local communities to develop alternative ways of earning a living that will not harm the environment, such as **low-impact** forestry and tourism.

*A Greenpeace forest campaigner visits Papua New Guinea villagers to talk about the consequences of logging in their district.*

Greenpeace lobbies groups such as governments and the World Bank to encourage changes in the way that timber industries operate. It also tries to persuade these groups to give aid money to environmentally sound projects rather than destructive ones, such as clear-felling. Greenpeace encourages people everywhere to avoid buying any paper or wood that comes from old-growth forests. If people do not buy these products, companies lose any reason to log old-growth forests.

Greenpeace is focusing on the issue of logging in old-growth forests because it is one of the few international campaigning organizations that can reach these isolated parts of the world.

## Classic action

The "Kids for Forests" campaign operates in 15 different countries. More than 1,000 children came to an important international United Nations conference in the Netherlands in 2002. They presented petitions signed by more than 240,000 people, calling for action.

# Climate change

Greenpeace is concerned that every day, all over the world, fossil fuels are used by millions of people for energy and transport. Many scientists believe that we damage our climate by using fossil fuels, because they produce gases that heat up the atmosphere. These are known as greenhouse gases. The build-up of greenhouse gases could affect our lives and destroy many natural environments in the future.

## CAMPAIGNS

Greenpeace believes that it makes environmental and economic sense to significantly reduce greenhouse pollution. It campaigns around the world to phase out the use of fossil fuels and tries to prevent dangerous climate change.

Greenpeace encourages everyone to use clean renewable energy such as solar, wind, and **hydropower**. These fuels will never run out, and do not have the same negative effects on the atmosphere that fossil fuels have. It also encourages people to use less fuel overall, and to petition their government to provide choices for renewable energy. Greenpeace also asks people to write letters to governments and company directors complaining that they do not do enough to prevent the build-up of greenhouse gases.

## Classic action

To publicize the "Choose Positive Energy" campaign, Greenpeace and the Body Shop held a dragon boat regatta in the Philippines. At the regatta, signatures were collected for a global petition against using fossil fuels as a source of energy.

*Dragon boats escort the* Rainbow Warrior *at the Philippines regatta.*

# Toxic damage

Greenpeace is concerned about the increasing use of **synthetic** chemicals to make the things we need. The synthetic chemicals that Greenpeace is particularly concerned about include pesticides, industrial chemicals, and the waste from incinerators. Some of these chemicals can cause serious problems to people's health and to the environment.

*Greenpeace activists protest outside a toxic waste site.*

CAMPAIGNS

Polyvinyl chloride, or PVC, is one example of a common form of chemical pollution. PVC is used in many building products, toys, shoes, luggage, and even paper. PVC gives off dangerous fumes when burned, and lasts for many years in landfill.

Greenpeace has a four-part campaign to stop the problems caused by synthetic chemicals:

1. Reduce all waste as much as possible, and eventually reuse or recycle all waste in some way.

2. Use alternatives like concrete, metal, and timber in building, and use recycled paper that is treated without chlorine bleaches.

3. Use methods of destroying synthetic chemical products that do not produce dangerous waste products themselves.

4. Use clean production methods in industries, such as using renewable, safe materials and efficient energy sources.

## Classic action

In the United States of America, Greenpeace encouraged people to write to well-known businesswoman Martha Stewart asking her to avoid packaging her homeware products in PVC.

*Glossary word*

**synthetic**
artificial, made by humans

# The health of the world's oceans

Greenpeace is concerned about the health of the world's oceans. Over-fishing, whaling, and pollution all cause great damage to oceans. Some species of marine life are at risk of becoming extinct and are in urgent need of protection.

## CAMPAIGNS

Two-thirds of the Earth's surface is made up of oceans. Greenpeace has campaigned for many years to stop all commercial whaling. This has been partly successful, as there is now a worldwide ban on commercial whaling. Unfortunately, though, despite this ban, some countries such as Japan, Norway, and Iceland still carry out either commercial whaling or what they call **scientific whaling**.

Greenpeace campaigns against over-fishing to try to protect marine species from probable extinction. The southern bluefin tuna and the Patagonian toothfish are two species that are in danger. Animals that depend on these fish as their food source are also put at risk of starvation. Other fish are also sometimes caught and drown in fishing lines used in commercial fishing. Greenpeace encourages people not to buy endangered fish from shops or restaurants, and calls for governments to protect fishing areas.

Greenpeace also campaigns against the uncontrolled shrimp-farming industry in developing countries. Uncontrolled shrimp-farming practices can damage the water with chemicals and fertilizers.

*Greenpeace activists try to stop a ship from taking a recently killed minke whale on board.*

### Glossary words

**scientific whaling**
catching whales for scientific investigation rather than to make money

**nature-based tourism**
tourism based on the natural, unspoiled environment

## Classic action

Greenpeace has suggested that it will help Iceland to set up a **nature-based tourism** program to bring in money if whaling is stopped.

# The increasing number of wars and conflicts

Greenpeace is concerned about the increasing number of wars and conflicts throughout the world. It believes that war is never the answer to any problem, and results in devastating human and environmental consequences.

## CAMPAIGNS

Greenpeace has always campaigned for world peace. In 2003, for example, there was massive global action against the war in Iraq. Greenpeace worked with a total of 47 non-governmental organizations to hold World Peace Now rallies around the world. Greenpeace used its flagship, the *Rainbow Warrior*, to blockade a military port in England and stop the loading of military supplies, until it was impounded by the government. E-mail campaigns and hot-air balloons were also used to create publicity, and peace symbols were projected onto the Sydney Opera House in Australia and the USS *Blue Ridge* in Hong Kong Harbour.

Another major peace campaign is against the Star Wars Missile Defense Program in the United States of America. Greenpeace is trying to convince people that the Star Wars program does not work and wastes billions of dollars. Greenpeace believes that this program will only lead to an increase in the use and supply of arms, and that it will prevent nuclear disarmament.

## Classic action

In Australia in April 2003, a length of rope, marked by buoys, balloons, and activists was spread across an exit channel from Sydney Harbour. This was meant to indicate that the HMAS *Sydney* should not be going to war.

*During the 2003 protest, two Greenpeace activists managed to board the HMAS* Sydney *from one of two small boats.*

# The people of Greenpeace

Greenpeace helps people and communities all over the world. Here are four volunteers who use their own specialized skills to help in different situations.

## CLEMENS TOLUSSO  Toxics campaigner

*Clemens Tolusso works hard to help Greenpeace make a difference in the world.*

Clemens Tolusso left an interesting job in the IT section of a bookselling firm to work with Greenpeace in Zurich, Switzerland, in 1993. Although his previous job was easier, and in fact better paid, he has never regretted his choice. He speaks French, German, and English, which makes him very useful as a press officer and translator, and has an active part in the toxics campaign.

In 1994, for example, he and other activists occupied a huge cave in a lime mine in the Swiss mountains. The Swiss government had allowed hazardous waste to be used as landfill in the mine. The mine was just above an important river used for drinking water. After the Greenpeace activists had occupied the mine for three weeks, the government reevaluated and eventually stopped the landfill project.

Another Greenpeace action in which Clemens was involved forced an aluminum company to clean up the dangerous waste in their landfill. It cost the company 20 million Swiss francs (that is more than $20 million Australian, or $15 million US).

In 2001 in Stockholm, Sweden, with the help of the United Nations, over 91 countries signed a global treaty calling for the elimination of Persistent Organic Pollutants (POPs), starting with the 12 worst, known as the "dirty dozen."

In another even more expensive action in 2000, Clemens and other Greenpeace activists occupied a landfill site where Swiss chemical industries dumped their waste products. As a result of the Greenpeace action, the industries involved have since cleaned the site at a cost of approximately 300 million Swiss francs!

As a part of his ongoing work with Greenpeace, Clemens will also continue to protest against nuclear weapons and the American Star Wars Missile Defense program.

Clemens is not confident that Greenpeace will be able to stop all of the negative effects humans have on the Earth. He uses his own family as an example. While they believe he is doing a good job, they also find it hard to change their familiar behaviors that are damaging the planet for future generations. Clemens will continue his work though, as he believes it is a matter of honor, and his duty, to fight against the destruction of the environment, and for peace in the world.

Did you know?

Over 30,000 chemicals are currently marketed in quantities over one ton, and that is just within the European Union!

*Clemens and other Greenpeace activists protested outside this Swiss landfill site against the dumping of chemical waste products.*

## VANESSA ATKINSON Climate campaigner

*Vanessa and another Greenpeace activist chain themselves to a ship containing genetically modified food.*

Vanessa is 28 years old and has been passionate about the environment for as long as she can remember. She studied environmental science at the University of New South Wales, Australia, and took up scuba diving while working on her degree. The dives led Vanessa to develop a particular interest in protecting the ocean and all of its wonderful and bizarre marine life.

After finishing school, Vanessa became a volunteer, then a paid worker for The Wilderness Society, an environmental protection group that was working to protect the Great Barrier Reef from destructive prawn trawling.

In 2000, Vanessa joined Greenpeace. She worked as an activist, helping to protect southern bluefin tuna from over-fishing. There are not many of this species left and they need to be protected. Vanessa has also worked on several other Greenpeace campaigns, including ones to prevent commercial whaling.

Enough sunlight hits the Earth every hour to supply the world with solar energy for a year.

Although she is based in New Zealand, Vanessa has traveled the world working on Greenpeace campaigns. She has attended an international fisheries meeting in Japan to convince several governments to stop fishing for southern bluefin tuna. In Italy, she attended a United Nations meeting on climate change.

Vanessa has taken part in some dramatic actions in her attempts to improve the environment. For 14 hours, Vanessa and other Greenpeace activists occupied a mine producing **shale oil** in Queensland, Australia. They were protesting against the mine contributing to dangerous climate change and impacting upon the Great Barrier Reef.

In March 2003, Vanessa and several other activists spent 21 hours chained to a huge overhead crane on a cargo ship in Melbourne, Australia. They wanted to prevent the unloading of genetically modified food from the ship's hold.

Vanessa thinks carefully before taking part in these sorts of actions. Greenpeace teaches its members ways to protest safely and efficiently, and encourages them to negotiate peacefully. They know that what they are doing is serious, and can mean being in tense situations for many hours with no sleep and little food. Like many other Greenpeace members, Vanessa is prepared to do this to stand up for the environment. She is encouraged by the success of many of the campaigns Greenpeace has worked on and by the support of her family.

At present, Vanessa is continuing her work in New Zealand, encouraging the government to create more renewable energy sources. This is part of the global fight to prevent dangerous climate change.

*Greenpeace activists in Queensland protest against the effects of shale-oil mining.*

Did you know?

Southern bluefin tuna can swim up to 40 miles per hour. They are the cheetahs of the ocean!

Glossary word

**shale oil**
oil that is obtained from rock containing bitumen

25

## HENRY TINDIPE  Forest campaigner

*This forest campaign focussed on the Paradise Forests of Papua New Guinea.*

Henry Tindipe grew up in Papua New Guinea. He now works to save his country's environment by stopping people from cutting down rainforest trees. While Greenpeace works to protect forests all over the world, at the moment Henry works only in the Australia–Pacific region.

The rain forests of Papua New Guinea have many huge, old trees. Many of the plants and animals that live there are found nowhere else. If the rain forests in Papua New Guinea disappear, these plants and animals could disappear too. The rain forests are also very important to the local people, who live in the forests or nearby. If the rain forests die, so does the locals' way of life.

Unfortunately, big trees can be worth a lot of money. Some logging companies have been stealing trees from Papua New Guinea's rain forests. They do this in areas far away from where people live, in the hope that no one will see them taking trees from the rain forests, because they don't want to get caught by the government.

Ten million hectares of old-growth forest are being cleared or destroyed every year. That's an area the size of a soccer field every two seconds.

Henry says, "These logging companies will do whatever they can to stop Greenpeace and others from telling the world what they are doing. I have been threatened, but I will not give up."

*Protesters take over a logging barge in Papua New Guinea to try to stop the export of rain forest timber.*

As a part of his work for Greenpeace, Henry sometimes travels to places like Japan. He tries to persuade people not to buy the logs from threatened areas. Sometimes he meets with other people who work with Greenpeace. But the time that Henry spends in the rain forests is the most valuable. He visits villages and talks to people there about what is going on around them. They tell Henry how the logging is threatening their way of life, and Henry tells all this to Greenpeace. Henry's work in the rain forests gives Greenpeace the facts they need to take action against illegal logging.

For six days in 2002, Greenpeace stopped a company from loading logs onto their ship. Greenpeace activists sat on the ship so the logs could not be loaded. This action was broadcast on the news and people around the world learned about illegal logging in Papua New Guinea.

The fight against illegal logging is ongoing. With help from people like Henry, maybe the rain forests can be saved.

Did you know?

Eighty percent of the world's old-growth forests have already disappeared.

*Louise Edge with other Greenpeace activists after a forest action.*

Louise joined Greenpeace while still at school. She began working for them as a press officer in 2000. It was her dream job! As a child, her love of nature made her concerned about environmental issues, and she believed that Greenpeace was an organization that could actually make a difference. Louise also enjoyed the exciting ways in which Greenpeace used the media to communicate its messages.

The most memorable action Louise has been involved in was at Menwith Hill, in the north of England. Menwith Hill is an American base that checks on telephone and fax communications in Europe. It is also used in the planning of the Star Wars Missile Defense program. One hundred peace activists, dressed as missiles, waddled through the gates of Menwith Hill as part of a protest against the work done at the base. Publicity about the protest was broadcast around the world. Greenpeace used humor and nonviolent action to tell people that it believed the Star Wars system was expensive, might not even work and could encourage more nuclear arms.

Did you know?

The Star Wars Missile Defense program is said to be costing the American government a total of more than $100 billion.

Louise finds her work with Greenpeace inspiring. Greenpeace lets people know about the problems facing the world and also works to provide practical solutions. Louise knows that she cannot change the world by herself, but as a part of Greenpeace, she can help to make a difference.

Louise understands that when people work for a cause they feel passionate about, they can sometimes feel that no matter how much they do, it will never be enough. Activists can be away from home for many months at a time working on campaigns, which can be hard on their families who are left behind. Luckily, Louise's family is supportive of the work she does to help protect the environment. Louise would like to take a break sometime soon and spend time with her family, and visit some of the beautiful parts of the world that she has helped to protect.

Did you know?

In 2001, there were at least 36,000 nuclear weapons in the world.

*Greenpeace volunteers occupy Menwith Hill as part of an international campaign to stop the Star Wars Missile Defense program.*

# What can you do?

Everybody, no matter how young or old, can work to help our environment. Greenpeace has many suggestions to help you get started.

## Learn about the Earth

Learn all you can about the Earth and the things that help and harm it. Libraries and conservation organizations have a lot of information. On the Greenpeace website at *www.greenpeace.org* you can take a virtual tour of an old-growth forest or find out about whaling.

## Save energy

Save energy whenever you can. To keep warm in winter, wear a jacket and keep the doors closed. If you are choosing a power source, think about renewable energy such as solar power.

## Write letters

Write letters or send postcards to politicians and businesses asking them to make good decisions that protect the environment. Greenpeace can help you decide whom to contact.

## Become a cyberactivist

Become a cyberactivist. This means using your computer to learn about environmental issues, inform others, and put pressure on those who cause harm to the Earth.

## Product usage

Be aware of the products you buy and use. Make sure that they are not causing any harm to the environment.

*Visit the Greenpeace website for information, campaign updates, and to find out how you can help.*

# Glossary

| | |
|---|---|
| activists | people who take direct action for a cause |
| ecology | the science of living things and their surroundings |
| empowered | given the power to make something happen |
| fossil fuels | sources of energy from the ground, such as coal, gas, and oil |
| genetically modified organisms | living things that have had their genetic structure changed |
| glacial retreat | the increased melting of glaciers due to climate change |
| global warming | the gradual increase in temperatures across the Earth, largely caused by too much carbon dioxide in the atmosphere |
| humanitarian | devoted to people's welfare and the promotion of social reform |
| human rights | a set of rights, such as the right to a fair trial, laid down by the United Nations |
| hydropower | power generated by the movement of water |
| International Whaling Commission | the international group of governments responsible for protecting whales and managing whaling |
| lobby | to attempt to convince government, business, or other powerful groups to change their policy or practices |
| low-impact | having a minimal effect on the environment |
| nature-based tourism | tourism based on the natural, unspoiled environment |
| nuclear disarmament | removal of all nuclear weapons and the facilities that make them |
| renewable energy | an energy source that will not run out, such as sunlight or wind |
| reprocessing | separation of plutonium from used-up nuclear fuel |
| scientific whaling | catching whales for scientific investigation rather than to make money |
| shale oil | oil that is obtained from rock containing bitumen |
| synthetic | artificial, made by humans |
| volunteers | people who donate their time to a cause |

## A

activists 5, 6, 14, 15, 21, 22–9

## B

bearing witness 6, 9, 10

## C

climate change 5, 13, 14, 18, 24–5
consumer boycotts 17, 20, 27, 30
core values 10–11

## D

direct action 5, 10, 22–5, 27, 28
donations 4, 14
Don't Make a Wave Committee 8, 13

## E

endangered species 6, 17, 20, 26

## F

fossil fuels 14, 18, 25

## G

genetically modified organisms 14, 16, 25

## H

history 5–9, 13

## I

independence 10
International Whaling Commission 7, 13

## L

letter-writing campaigns 18, 19, 21, 30
locations 12–13
logging 13, 14, 17, 26–7

## M

membership 7, 8, 9, 14

## N

nonviolence 5, 10, 28
nuclear disarmament 14, 21
nuclear reactors 15
nuclear testing 6, 7, 8–9, 11, 13, 15
nuclear weapons 5, 6, 7, 14, 15, 21, 28, 29

## O

oceans 20, 24
old-growth forests 14, 17, 26–7, 30
over-fishing 14, 20, 24

## P

peaceful protests 10, 25, 28
pollution 7, 18, 20
publicity 5, 6, 9, 11, 18, 21, 27, 28

## R

*Rainbow Warrior* 7, 13, 21
rain forests 17, 26–7
renewable energy 14, 18, 25, 30

## S

seal hunting 7
Star Wars Missile Defense Program 21, 23, 28
sustainable development 11

## T

timeline 13
toxic chemicals 13, 14, 19, 22–3
toxic waste 7, 14, 15, 19, 22–3

## U

United Nations 13, 17, 22, 24

## W

war 21
whaling 7, 13, 14, 20, 24, 30
wildlife conservation 6, 13, 20, 24, 26